My Heart Will ~~Go~~ On
& 9 more great movie love songs

CONTENTS

Production: Sadie Cook

Published 1998

IMP

© International Music Publications Limited
Southend Road, Woodford Green, Essex IG8 8HN, England

DON'T BE
A MUSIC
COPYCAT!

The copying of © copyright
material is a criminal offence
and may lead to prosecution.

Because You Loved Me

**Words and Music by
Diane Warren**

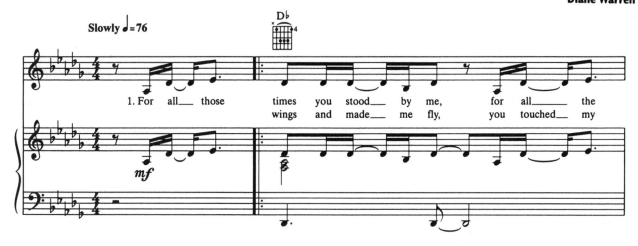

4

6

(Everything I Do) I Do It For You

Words and Music by Bryan Adams,
Robert John 'Mutt' Lange and Michael Kamen

VERSE 2:
Look into your heart
You will find there's nothin' there to hide
Take me as I am, take my life
I would give it all, I would sacrifice.

Don't tell me it's not worth fightin' for
I can't help it, there's nothin' I want more
You know it's true, everything I do
I do it for you.

A Groovy Kind Of Love

**Words and Music by
Toni Wine and Carole Bayer-Sager**

I Will Always Love You

Words and Music by
Dolly Parton

Verse 3: Instrumental solo

Verse 4:
I hope life treats you kind
And I hope you have all you've dreamed of.
And I wish to you, joy and happiness.
But above all this, I wish you love.
(To Chorus:)

In All The Right Places

Words and Music by John Barry, Lisa Stansfield, Ian Devaney and Andy Morris

VERSE 2:
If we're dancing all alone
Or in a crowded room,
When you wrap your arms around me,
You always send me to the moon.
When we kiss our sugar kisses,
And the music starts to play,
We've got love, we've got each other
And we're going all the way.

189 - EQUINOX.
ACMP VOL 15.

24

My Heart Will Go On
(Love Theme from "Titanic")

Words by Will Jennings
Music by James Horner

Summer Nights

**Words and Music by
Warren Casey and Jim Jacobs**

Take My Breath Away

Words by Tom Whitlock
Music by Giogio Moroder

Verse 2:
Watching, I keep waiting, still anticipating love,
Never hesitating to become the fated ones.
Turning and returning to some secret place to hide;
Watching in slow motion as you turn my way and say,
"Take my breath away." *(To Bridge:)*

Verse 3:
Watching every motion in this foolish lover's game;
Haunted by the notion somewhere's there's a love in flames.
Turning and returning to some secret place inside;
Watching in slow motion as you turn to me and say,
"Take my breath away." *(To Coda:)*

Tears In Heaven

**Words and Music by Eric Clapton
and Will Jennings**

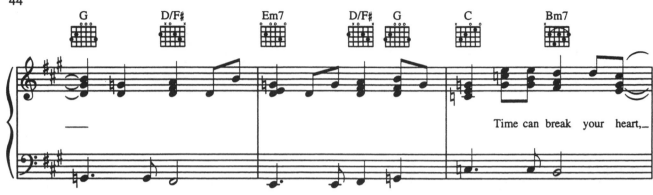

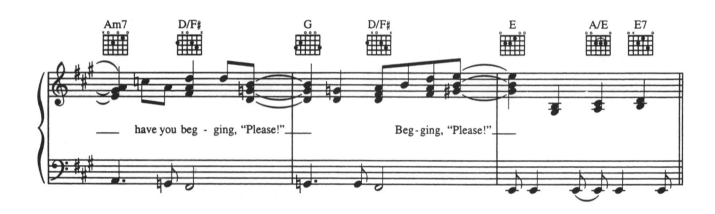

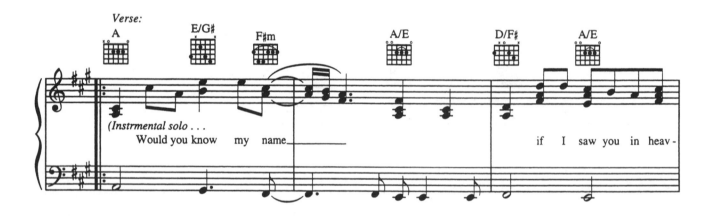

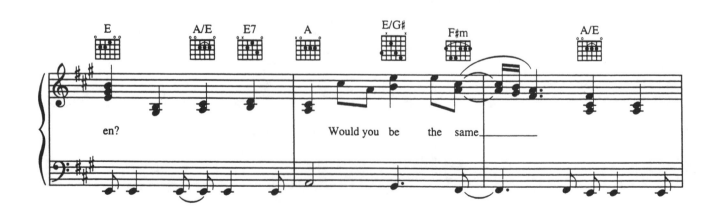

The Wind Beneath My Wings

**Words and Music by
Larry Henley and Jeff Silbar**

It must have been cold__ there__ in my shad - ow,

to nev - er have sun - light on your face.

You've been con - tent__ to let me shine,

you al-ways walked___ the step be - hind.___

I was the one___ with all the glo - ry,

while you were the one___ with all the strength,

on - ly a face___ with-out a name,

The All Woman Series

All Woman
volume one

Contents include: All Woman; Do You Know Where You're Going To?; Ev'ry Time We Say Goodbye;
Fever; I Am What I Am; I Will Always Love You; Miss You Like Crazy; Summertime;
Superwoman; What's Love Got To Do With It and Why Do Fools Fall In Love.
Order Ref: 19076

All Woman
volume two

Contents include: Don't It Make My Brown Eyes Blue; Giving You The Best That I Got;
Killing Me Softly With His Song; Memory; One Moment In Time; Pearl's A Singer;
That Ole Devil Called Love; Walk On By; The Wind Beneath My Wings and You Don't Have To Say You Love Me.
Order Ref: 2043A

All Woman
volume three

Contents include: Almaz; Big Spender; Crazy For You; Fame; The First Time Ever I Saw Your Face;
From A Distance; Love Letters; My Baby Just Cares For Me; My Funny Valentine; The Power Of Love;
Promise Me; Saving All My Love For You and Total Eclipse Of The Heart.
Order Ref: 2444A

All Woman
volume four

Contents include: Anything For You; Evergreen; For Your Eyes Only; I Will Survive; Mad About The Boy;
A Rainy Night in Georgia; Send In The Clowns; Smooth Operator; Sophisticated Lady; Stay With Me Till Dawn;
Sweet Love; Think Twice and Touch Me In The Morning.
Order Ref: 3034A

All Woman
Blues

Contents include: Body and Soul; Georgia On My Mind; God Bless' The Child;
I Don't Stand A Ghost Of A Chance With You; I Gotta Right To Sing The Blues; I'd Rather Go Blind;
Lover Man (Oh, Where Can You Be?); Mood Indigo; Stormy Weather and You've Changed.
Order Ref: 3690A

All Woman
Cabaret

Contents include: Almost Like Being In Love; Another Openin', Another Show; Anything Goes;
For Once In My Life; Goldfinger; I Won't Last A Day Without You; If My Friends Could See Me Now;
My Way; New York New York; People and There's No Business Like Show Business.
Order Ref: 3691A

All Woman
Jazz

Contents include: Bewitched; Crazy He Calls Me; A Foggy Day; Girl From Ipanema; How High The Moon;
I'm In The Mood For Love; It Don't Mean A Thing (If It Ain't Got That Swing); It's Only A Paper Moon;
Misty; On Green Dolphin Street; 'Round Midnight and Straighten Up And Fly Right.
Order Ref: 4778A